Jules Massenet

Méditation
from *Thaïs*

Transcribed for piano by Andrew von Oeyen

ALPHONSE
LEDUC
ÉDITIONS MUSICALES

AL 30 878

Méditation from *Thaïs*

Jules Massenet
Transcribed for piano by Andrew von Oeyen

AL 30 878

*Tous droits d'exécution, de reproduction,
de transcription et d'adaptation réservés pour tous pays*